Cartooning for Kids!

Furry & Feathered Friends

By Dave Garbot

©2014 Quarto Publishing Group USA Inc.

Published by Walter Foster Jr., an imprint of Quarto Publishing Group USA Inc.

All rights reserved. Walter Foster Jr. is trademarked.

Publisher: Rebecca J. Razo

Creative Director: Shelley Baugh

Project Editor: Janessa Osle

Senior Editor: Stephanie Meissner

Managing Editor: Karen Julian

Associate Editor: Jennifer Gaudet

Production Artists: Debbie Aiken, Amanda Tannen

Production Manager: Nicole Szawlowski

Production Coordinator: Lawrence Marquez

Illustrated and written by Dave Garbot

www.walterfoster.com

3 Wrigley, Suite A

Irvine, CA 92618

1 3 5 7 9 10 8 6 4 2

Table of Contents

What You Will Need

crayons

eraser

colored pencils

markers

pencil

Drawing paper

Getting Started

Now that you have everything you need, we're ready to go. Even if this is your first time drawing, this will be a lot of fun and something you can do over and over again. The most important thing to remember is to have fun! The more you smile, the happier your furry and feathered friends will be! Grab your pencil and paper and dive right in!

Funny Features

Here are a few basic features you can use when drawing furry and feathered animals. Use this section for ideas if you want to give your character a different look.

Ears

Tails

Eyes

Noses & Beaks

Feet

9

Accessories

Sometimes characters like to dress up or carry funny objects with them. Here are some ideas for snazzy accessories you can use.

Cute & Cuddly

In this section we'll draw characters that are just too cute—they're guaranteed to make you smile! As you draw these cute and cuddly animals, think of how sweet they are, and maybe you can add an accessory or two to make them even more adorable!

Bun-Bun

This bunny has his eyes closed. Can you draw him with his eyes open? Hint: Try making your rectangle a little wider at the top in step 1.

Porky

Can you draw Porky without a hat?
It's ok if your shapes and lines are wiggly!

Perry Penguin

This penguin is all set for chilly weather, but how would he look with sunglasses or a sombrero? Also, do you know what penguins eat? Go back to page 11 and pick out a snack!

Digger

Digger looks pretty spiffy in his jacket. Can you change the colors and patterns on his clothes? How would Digger look with different eyes?

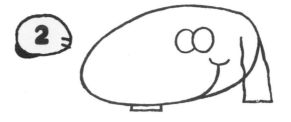

21

Kit Cat

Adding the extra lines shown in step 2 will create this kitty's football-shaped head. Can you add more bells to her collar?

23

Feather Frenzy

In this section we'll draw some of our favorite feathered friends. Birds come in all sizes and colors—especially cartoon birds—so have fun and experiment! Feel free to change up their clothes or the colors of their feathers. They won't mind at all!

Henrietta

Whoa...those are some crazy socks and shoes! Can you add a hat? Start your drawing with simple rectangles, and then use your eraser to give Henrietta her shape.

Chirp!

1

2

3

4

5

6

chirp!

27

Hoots

Hoots looks like he needs company. Make the branch longer and give him some friends! Maybe you can try a different pattern for his feathers.

29

Ellie Ostrich

Can you draw this lady ostrich without her shoes? Would she have toes? Don't worry if your circles in steps 1 and 2 aren't perfect—it's ok if they are a little wobbly.

Pelican Pete

This pelican has a mouse in his hat. Can you draw a few little birds up there instead?

Tommy Toucan

This is one happy toucan. Can you make a second bird that is much smaller? Just follow the same steps!

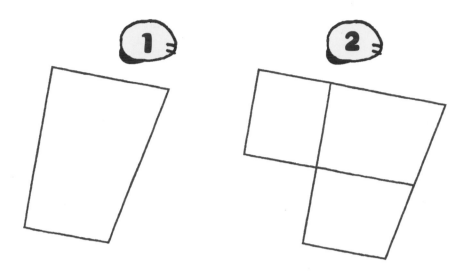

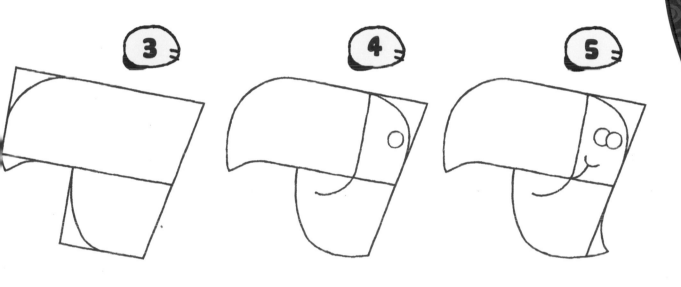

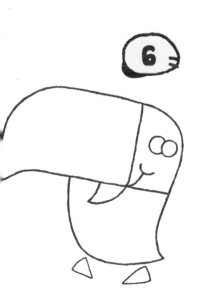

Forest Friends

In this section we'll draw furry friends that are usually found in the forest or somewhere else in the great outdoors. Even though these critters live outside, they still like to dress up. So don't forget to give your animals a hat or a tie to pair with their fur coats!

Billy Beaver

Billy is cute and cuddly just the way he is, but how would he look with a hat from page 11? Try it out and see!

38

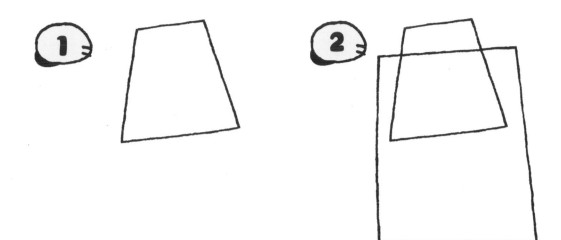

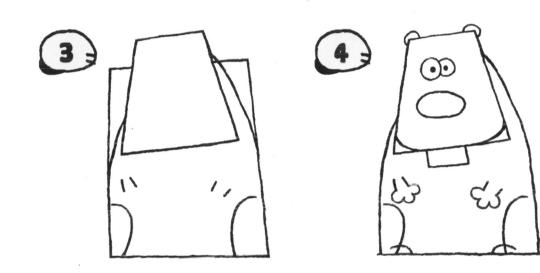

FOXY

This fox is really cute. Can you give her an adorable hat to wear? Start your drawing with an upside-down triangle with a slightly rounded top.

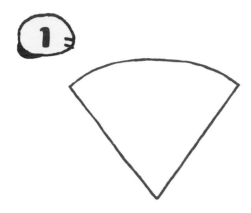

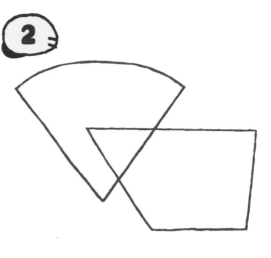

Milton Moose

Should Milton have more bird friends, or fewer? You decide! To draw his head, start with a pear-like shape that isn't quite oval.

Scout

Scout looks happy with his big acorn. Can you give him a cheesy grin? Maybe change the acorn to something else—how about an apple?

45

Smelly Skunk

Not all skunks are black and white. Can you change the color of this smelly friend's fur to something unique and different?

Ralph Raccoon

Have you ever seen a blue raccoon? Try out some different colors for this critter, or create a new pattern for his tie. Can you draw him facing the other way? Hint: follow the same steps, but draw his head facing left and his tail facing right.

1

2

3

4

5

6

49

Wild Wonders

You probably won't see any of the animals in this section roaming around in your neighborhood, but they are still fun to draw wearing clothes and accessories. Have you ever seen a cow in a dress or a koala with sunglasses? Anything is possible with the wild, wacky creatures in this group!

Percy Panda

Pandas are usually black and white, but if you use your imagination, this one can be blue, yellow, or even pink!

Greta

Greta is ready for spring, but where did those crazy chicks come from? Can you make Greta taller?
Hint: Make all of the shapes longer.

3

Henry Hippo

This hippo is a pretty shade of yellow, but you can change his color (and the color of his spots) if you want. How about blue, pink, or green? Mix and match as many color combinations as you can think of!

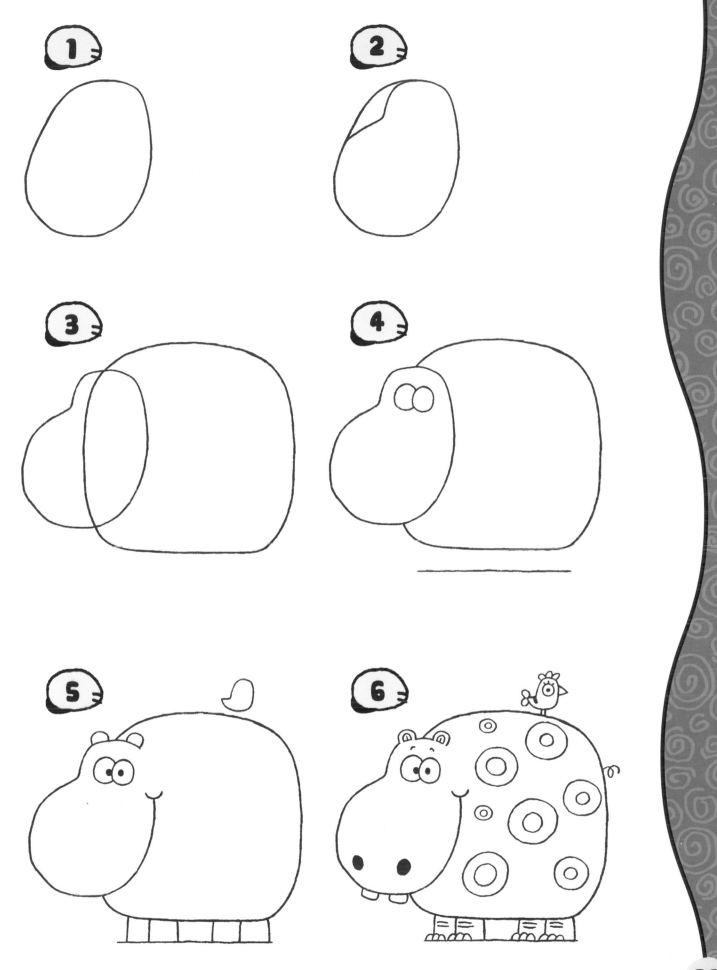

Wally Walrus

This walrus is taking a relaxing break on his rock. Can you add the sun shining down on him and a few more fish in the water?

1

2

3

4

5

6

7

Kool Koala

This koala is one cool dude. How would he look with different ears and a crazy tail? Go back to pages 8-9 if you need any ideas.

ROO

Can you give our friend Roo more than one buddy to carry in her pouch?

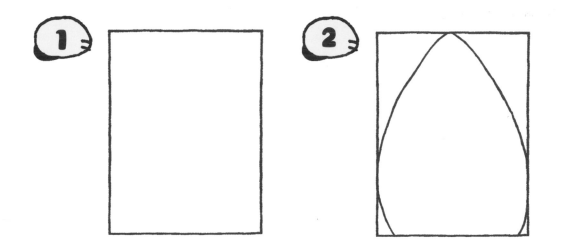

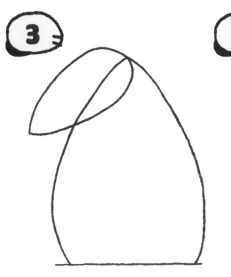

About the Author

Dave Garbot is a professional illustrator and has been drawing for as long as he can remember. He is frequently called upon to create characters for children's books and other publications. Dave always has a sketchbook with him, and he gets many of his ideas from the things he observes every day, as well as from lots of colorful childhood memories. Although he admits that creating characters brings him personal enjoyment, making his audience smile, feel good, and maybe even giggle is what really makes his day.

Dave is from Portland, Oregon, and you can see more of his work at www.garbot.com.